WINTER'S ORPHANS

The Search for a Family of Mountain Lion Cubs

A TRUE STORY

Robert C. Farentinos

Illustrated by Shannon Keegan

ROBERTS RINEHART PUBLISHERS

I dedicate this book to the "Teekster,"

my loyal companion and friend.

—R.C.F.

For my mother and father.

—S.K.

Text copyright © 1993 by Robert C. Farentinos
Artwork copyright © 1993 by Shannon Keegan

Published in the United States by Roberts Rinehart Publishers,
121 Second Avenue, Niwot, Colorado 80544

Library of Congress Cataloging-in-Publication Data
Farentinos, Robert C., 1941-
　　Winter's Orphans : the search for a family of mountain lion cubs,
　　a true story / Robert C. Farentinos ; illustrated by Shannon Keegan.
　　p. cm.
　　"A Rhino Book."
　　Includes bibliographical references (p. 64).
　　Summary : The author, a wildlife biologist, describes how he helped find the orphaned cubs of a mountain lion
　　shot near his home in Colorado and how the cubs were cared for until they could be released back into the wild.
　　ISBN 1-879373-40-8 (cloth) : ISBN 1-879373-53-X (paper)
　　1. Pumas – Colorado – Juvenile literature.　2. Wildlife rescue -
　　- Colorado –Juvenile literature.　[1. Pumas – Colorado.　2. Wildlife rescue.]
　　I. Keegan, Shannon, ill.　II. Title.
QL737.C23F37　1993
599.74'428 – dc20
                                                                                     92-61906
                                                                                          CIP
                                                                                          AC

Acknowledgments

With great appreciation I acknowledge the help of St. Anton residents Kristi Weaver, Linda Hurth, Lauren Ward and Fred Rodak; Colorado Division of Wildlife officials Jerry Apker, Kristi Coughlin and Kathi Greene; wildlife rehabilitation center owners Cece and Tom Sanders; writer Bonnie Garmus, Kevin Hansen of the Mountain Lion Foundation, Craig Pugh of the Brookfield Zoo and Chris Wemmer of the Smithsonian Institution for reading and commenting on the story; and Danièle Arnaud, who provided valuable assistance in the field. I especially want to thank Shannon Keegan for her superlative illustrations, endless encouragement and heroic patience with me.

For tens of thousands of years, the steep canyons and towering rim rocks along the Front Range of the Rocky Mountains have been the favored haunts of the mountain lion. Here, with the help of other large predators like the bear and the wolf, the mountain lion has played an important role in preserving the balance of nature.

Since at least the passing of the last Ice Age over ten thousand years ago, humans have shared the same environment with this magnificent carnivore. As top predators in the food web, both the mountain lion and early North Americans occupied crucial positions in the ecosystem. Often in direct competition for certain food sources, mountain lions and humans still managed to coexist for hundreds of centuries.

Then about the beginning of the seventeenth century, new visitors from distant lands began to arrive. Among the first to come were Spanish soldiers and explorers; they brought horses and domesticated animals with them. Soon to follow were the fur trappers, miners and settlers, who staked out farms and ranches throughout the Colorado region. It was not too long before towns and cities began to spring up. And more and more people moved into areas along the foothills of the Rockies to build their homes and enjoy the beauty of the natural surroundings.

This great migration of people meant that it would eventually become difficult for humans and mountain lions to keep out of each other's way. The large number of farm animals and pets suddenly roaming the "neighborhood" were tempting snacks for this swift and powerful predator. From a stray sheep or billy goat to a pen full of chickens and geese, the mountain lion occasionally helped itself to someone's livestock or worse, the family pet.

For some people, catching a glimpse of a mountain lion bounding through an open forest of ponderosa pine is a rare and wonderful wildlife experience, forever to be remembered. They argue that the mountain lion has a rightful place in the ecosystem. They also say that humans have disturbed the ecology of the foothills by introducing new species of animals and by planting exotic shrubs and gardens, which attract more deer, in turn attracting more mountain lions. As the so-called "intelligent species," it is up to us to figure out how we can alter our behavior to live in peace with the mountain lion, as well as all other creatures.

For other people, the mere thought of a big cat anywhere in the near vicinity is enough to send them scrambling for their rifles.

This story is about a mountain lion family that lived in the foothills just west of Boulder, Colorado, in an area called St. Anton Highlands. It is based on an actual event that happened during the winter of 1991. In telling this story, I hope to give a glimpse of the mountain lion's rapidly changing world; a world in which this majestic mammal is being continually challenged by the civilized needs of humans.

Robert C. Farentinos
Spring, 1992

5

One cold January evening, I had just lit a fire in the potbelly stove of my mountain cabin and flipped on the TV to catch the evening news. Tiki, my big black dog—a hundred-pound cross between a Rottweiler and Golden Retriever—took his usual position next to the stove.

The newscaster, much to my surprise, announced that there had been another mountain lion incident in the foothills west of Boulder. Sorrowfully, this one ended with the mountain lion being shot.

Suddenly, the camera switched to the scene of the shooting. Standing next to his pickup was a tall man wearing a cowboy hat. He was pointing to the lifeless body of a mountain lion stretched out on the bed of the truck. The man explained how he had no choice but to shoot the mountain lion because it was going after his chickens and geese.

According to him, it was about five o'clock in the afternoon of the previous day when he happened to look out his kitchen window and saw the mountain lion stalking one of his hens. He hurriedly grabbed a pistol from his gun cabinet and went outside to confront the mountain lion, which stopped abruptly and just sat there staring at him from about fifty feet away. So he carefully aimed the pistol and fired at the cat. It jumped up off the ground a couple of feet, ran over to a thicket of aspen and collapsed.

I was disturbed by the seemingly insensitive way the man described the incident. He kept saying how he had no alternative but to shoot the mountain lion in order to protect his domestic animals. I kept wondering if there might have been something else he could have done short of killing it.

As the reporter at the scene commented about how interactions between humans and mountain lions were becoming more and more frequent along the Colorado Front Range, the camera panned the immediate surroundings.

A broken-down plywood shelter housing two horses came into view. Bales of hay covered by a blue plastic tarp were piled next to the makeshift barn. Some of the bales had toppled from the pile and had broken open. In front of the barn were two wrecked cars; next to the main house itself were two other dilapidated vehicles. The garage was jammed with pieces of metal and trash, which spilled out into the driveway. Litter of all types—plastic, Styrofoam, cardboard—was strewn everywhere. Busily foraging through all of the mess were some free-ranging chickens and a couple of large geese.

The scene looked very familiar to me, and when the reporter said that the shooting had taken place on Ridge Road near St. Anton Highlands, it suddenly clicked. I knew exactly where that property was located. I had driven past it plenty of times, and on several occasions I had to slow down or stop to avoid the chickens, which tended to include the center of Ridge Road as part of their home range.

The next day, curious to find out more details about what had happened, I called the main office of the Colorado Division of Wildlife in Denver. I spoke to the head wildlife manager for the district who told me that although the circumstances of the shooting were a bit suspect, there was really nothing the Division could do, because the law gives people the right to protect themselves and their livestock from large predators such as mountain lions, bears and coyotes. We both agreed that this particular shooting was unfortunate and was probably avoidable if the property owner had realized how his apparent misuse of the land may have contributed to the problem. Letting chickens, geese, and other barnyard animals run loose in a forest setting and allowing trash heaps to accumulate were sure ways of inviting unwanted predators into the area.

My conversation with the wildlife manager revealed that the dead mountain lion was a female. She weighed just under one hundred pounds and she had recently been nursing. Suspecting the presence of cubs, wildlife rangers were sent to search the nearby area. One of them discovered some mountain lion prints in a patch of snow—a large set belonging to the female and several smaller ones presumably belonging to the cubs.

Now the real extent of the tragedy became apparent. Somewhere out there in the forest, alone and inexperienced, was a litter of orphaned mountain lion cubs.

News of the shooting had quickly spread among the residents living in St. Anton. For them, as with myself, it was an extremely rare event to even see a wild mountain lion, let alone have one shot in a neighbor's back yard. A few of the residents expressed relief that another marauding beast had been dispatched, saving them and their families from any potential danger. But most felt differently about what had happened. They sensed a definite loss both to themselves and to the forest, and they wondered, as I did, if killing the mountain lion had really been the best solution.

Several days had passed since the shooting of the mother mountain lion, and concern for the welfare of the cubs began to mount. The cubs—four of them—had actually been sighted several times: Once by a man who saw them on his back porch next to the garbage bin. Another time, two women hiking along the rim of Boulder Canyon saw the cubs sunning themselves on some large rocks. And finally, a young boy came face to face with them not far from his house while he was out in the woods playing his favorite game of commando. Apparently the four cubs, an unusually large litter for mountain lions, were still alive and wandering about, but time was running out.

Fearing for the cubs' safety and survival, the wildlife authorities decided it would be best to capture them. The plan was to care for and protect the cubs until it was time to release them again in the wild.

One evening I was contacted by the district wildlife manager, who knew of my past experience as a field biologist. He asked if I would assist in trapping the cubs. Naturally, I agreed. In fact, I had already decided to spend the next week or so tracking the cubs in hopes of determining their exact whereabouts and their condition.

The next day a wildlife ranger drove up from Denver with a load of

large live-traps made of heavy wire mesh. The traps were really designed for raccoons, but were just about the right size for the cubs, who we estimated to be about three months old and weigh about twenty to twenty-five pounds each.

Tiki could tell that something very out of the ordinary was going on. He sniffed at the traps, which no doubt possessed some interesting odors of past occupants. As the ranger and I got in the truck to leave, Tiki realized that he was not going to be part of this particular expedition and got that typical so-I-have-to-stay-here-again look on his big black face. "Not this time, Mr. T," I explained, "you might see the cubs before we do and go chasing after them, and we can't have that."

We decided to set the traps not far from the mother lion's denning area, which had recently been discovered by two women from the neighborhood. The day before, the cubs had been spotted near the denning area by them. Carefully, we placed canned cat food in the traps as bait, and also smeared some rocks and old logs with the smelly stuff, hoping that the strong, fishy odor would attract the cubs to the area.

Because of the steep, rocky terrain, it took the ranger and me several hours to set all of the traps, even with the help of the two neighborhood women who had located one of the denning areas. After we finally finished, the ranger took off back to Denver and the two women returned home.

In hopes of finding some sign of the cubs, I decided to walk back to my cabin, heading east along the rim of the canyon paralleling the twisting ribbon of highway several hundred feet below.

I walked for about an hour along the south-facing ridge of the canyon. It was quarter past three in the afternoon when I looked at my watch. The January sun, low in the southern sky, favored the exposed slopes with its winter warmth. I climbed to a towering rise of granite and sat atop a large boulder to scan the area with my binoculars. Nothing but more rocks and more ponderosa.

I was ready to stand up and leave when I caught a glimpse of movement directly below me just a hundred feet or so. It was followed by another, and still another. I focused my binoculars for closer range and much to my surprise, partially hidden behind a fallen tree, a tiny round head with blue eyes and long white whiskers came into view. It was one of the cubs!

Elated at the discovery, my heart began to pound with excitement, so much so that I could hardly keep my field glasses trained on the subject. Suddenly, another cub emerged from behind a large bush, and then two others made their appearance. They had not detected me. So, I sat very quietly and watched them as they playfully ran and jumped over the rocky profile of the canyon wall.

They all appeared to be healthy, and they seemed in good spirits, frolicking about quite acrobatically. As the wildlife ranger had guessed, they seemed to be about three months old. The big brown spots so distinguishable on the coats of younger mountain lion cubs were fading. And, their strong and deliberate movements resembled those of adult cats rather than the awkward antics of kittens.

One of the cubs clearly stood out from the other three. It was noticeably larger and more robust. It also seemed to dominate the play with more aggressive gestures and attacks. I concluded from its size and behavior that it must be a male.

I watched the cubs intently for a good fifteen minutes when suddenly the large cub stopped and peered directly at me. I was discovered. He paused for a moment and then quickly ran off down the canyon. The other cubs followed.

Not wanting to alarm the cubs and drive them further toward the bottom of the canyon and the danger of the busy highway, I proceeded very slowly away from the area, marking in my mind the exact spot where this initial sighting had taken place. I would return tomorrow to this area to resume the tracking.

That evening as I sat in my cabin recounting to Tiki the day's events, I thought how lucky I had been to actually locate the cubs and to see my first mountain lions in the wild. They were all so exciting and fun to watch, but that one large cub was certainly the most impressive of the bunch. I decided to give him a name, something to commemorate the occasion of my first mountain lion sighting. So, I began to thumb through my little dictionary of word roots and combining forms, a reference for understanding biological terms and scientific names that I kept from my old college days.

"Ahah! here's one that'll do just fine, Mr. T," I exclaimed. "Lanthos, meaning hidden or unseen. Yes, this one's perfect. I'll call him Lanthito for short, the unseen one. Truly a name befitting his species, don't you think, Tiki?"

My initial enthusiasm of locating Lanthito and this littermates and my early optimism for trapping them began to diminish after several days of intense tracking with no sign of the cubs. The weather was still holding out, though—no big winter storms yet that could plummet the temperature to well below zero and drop a couple feet of snow.

I had questioned several of my neighbors to see if they had recently spotted the cubs. One man told of seeing the cubs licking the legs of his metal barbecue. I also received a chilling account from one woman, whose home was no more than two hundred yards from my cabin, of how she had watched in disbelief as an adult mountain lion attacked and killed her dog about two weeks earlier. No doubt it was Lanthito's mother, who was intent on feeding her cubs.

A few days later my despair in neither sighting nor trapping the cubs reached a new low. I received a telephone call from the wildlife ranger who told me that one of the cubs had been run over by a car down on the the canyon road. It was a small male—not Lanthito, I presumed. When they autopsied it, they found some dog remains in the cub's stomach. Apparently, the cubs were feeding on prey that the mother mountain lion had stashed away shortly before she had been shot.

It had been almost a week since the live-traps were put out. I had just returned home from checking and rebaiting them late in the evening.

As I sat in the warmth and security of my log cabin, I thought of Lanthito and his two littermates and wondered where they were and what they were doing. I tried to imagine what it would be like to actually be a mountain lion cub, like Lanthito, facing similar uncertainties and threats to my survival.

Other mammals besides ourselves certainly do have the capacity to think and to feel a wide range of emotions such as fear, anger, boredom, and anxiety. But it is impossible for us to know how closely these thoughts and feelings are to our own, even under similar circumstances. Nonetheless, it is interesting to speculate.

Impressions of Lanthito and the other cubs co-mingled with my ponderings about science and animal behavior, and reflections of past events—the shooting of Lanthito's mother, the discovery of the denning area, the neighbor who described the loss of her dog, the cub who was hit by a car. And, I wished I was able to jump into the mind of a mountain lion for just a little while.

I began to doze off and suddenly found myself in the most remarkable dream, the details of which are still quite vivid in my mind.

The loud crack of a gun shattered the stillness of the late afternoon. Lanthito lurched up from a restless slumber as the echo of the blast peeled off the sides of the sheer canyon walls and died slowly away with an eerie rumble.

Lanthito unraveled himself from the other three cubs, who remained asleep where their mother had left them for her evening hunt.

Puzzled and a bit alarmed, he listened carefully for a clue. Nothing but familiar noises—a mild breeze whistling through the pine needles, the cackling call of a Steller's jay, and the muffled roar of an auto filtering up from the canyon road a thousand feet below.

Lanthito jumped over to a large sun-lit boulder. Several minutes had passed since he was awakened by the big noise. The warm rock felt good and he stretched out on his belly to soak up the heat. The granite outcropping that formed the denning site faced the southern sky. Even in mid-winter it was bathed in sunshine for the better part of the day. And this January, the weather was especially mild.

Lanthito had just started to doze off again when he heard the shouts and chatter of humans coming from the same direction as the big noise. Lanthito was used to the sounds made by these gangling, two-legged creatures, although he had no idea about their meaning.

Not more than two hundred feet from the denning site, separated by a large jumble of lichen-covered boulders and a thick stand of ponderosa pine, stood a house and several outbuildings. From the well-concealed nooks and crannies of the boulders, Lanthito and his littermates often observed the behavior of the two-leggers and their odd assortment of animals.

There were some huge ones, bigger than the largest elk they had ever seen. They had no antlers and spent most of the day standing in one place and swishing their long tails back and forth. Occasionally a two-legger sat atop such a beast and together they would ramble through the forest.

And there were strange-looking birds. Some were all white and stood very tall. Their voices were loud and deep like a raven's. They had big yellow feet and their bottoms waddled as they walked. There were others with red feathers that made peculiar clucking sounds and were constantly pecking at the ground. They were a little larger than a blue grouse and hardly ever flew.

From their secret vantage points amidst the rock outcroppings, Lanthito and the other cubs would often watch their mother quietly stalk the redbirds. Crouching close to the snowy ground, her tensed body concealed by the dense underbrush, she would suddenly spring in a tawny blur and grab a redbird with her outstretched paws. It happened very quickly and silently in a puff of red feathers.

Lanthito and his littermates relished the redbirds that their mother brought back to the denning area. The redbirds were certainly as good as anything else they had eaten, and they seemed to be quite plentiful.

But mostly, Lanthito and the cubs fed upon their mother's kills of deer. She led them to the place where she hid her prey under a mound of dirt and pine needles, and there they would all feed until they became quite content. But never once had they seen how she managed to catch such big animals.

Lanthito remembered one winter evening just around dusk, when he and the other cubs accompanied their mother on a hunt. As they approached a group of houses she slowed her pace and gazed intently toward some noises coming from the rear of one of the buildings. Slowly and quietly she led the cubs to within a hundred feet of the house. With a muffled mew she ordered them to stop and stay put.

From their hiding place they could see a two-legger walking with one of its dogs. The two-legger tied the dog to a tree and then turned to enter the house. Suddenly Lanthito's mother dashed forward and pounced on top of the tethered canine. It let out a yelp and immediately fell silent under the powerful grip of the female mountain lion.

The back door of the house burst open and the two-legger began yelling loudly at Lanthito's mother, who sat guardedly over her prey. The two-legger ran back into the house and returned beating on a metal pan with a big spoon. All the clamor alarmed Lanthito and the other cubs, but they quietly remained crouched close to the ground where their mother had signaled them to stay.

As the two-legger came closer, Lanthito's mother stood up, and with ears menacingly flattened backward, she growled loudly. The two-legger stopped abruptly. Lanthito's mother grabbed the carcass between her powerful jaws and with a mighty tug ripped the rope away from the tree. Although the prey was nearly half her size, Lanthito's mother carried it off with apparent ease and headed swiftly back toward the awaiting cubs. With another mew-like sound, she signaled them to follow and they all made their way back into the forest, the stunned and no doubt terrified two-legger looking on from a distance.

These lucid flashes of memory locked deep inside Lanthito's storehouse of experience rapidly faded away as the reality of his situation once again revealed itself. By now, some time had passed since Lanthito was awakened by the big noise and he was beginning to get hungry. Below him the other cubs were stirring—they stretched and yawned and pawed at each other in play.

The sounds of the two-leggers' voices grew louder and Lanthito's curiosity increased. Earlier in the day, before she had departed, Lanthito's mother instructed him and the other cubs to remain at the denning site until she returned with food. Lanthito remembered the warning, but could not resist seeing what all the bother was about just on the other side of the boulder pile.

He climbed higher up the rock outcropping until he had a good view of the surrounding terrain and scanned in the direction of the two-leggers' voices.

From his position he could see several two-leggers standing close to his mother. She was stretched out on the ground as though she was

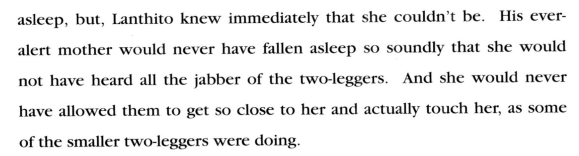

asleep, but, Lanthito knew immediately that she couldn't be. His ever-alert mother would never have fallen asleep so soundly that she would not have heard all the jabber of the two-leggers. And she would never have allowed them to get so close to her and actually touch her, as some of the smaller two-leggers were doing.

Lanthito felt a great urge to run over to his mother. But, he was frightened and perplexed by all that was going on. Then a couple of the two-leggers walked over to his mother and with great effort lifted her up. They clumsily carried her to a pickup truck and laid her limp and lifeless body on top of it.

The young cub watched intently, straining to see a sign from his mother but none appeared. He waited there for a long time not knowing what to do. Finally a couple of two-leggers threw ropes over Lanthito's mother and tied her down. Then one of the two-leggers got into the truck and started it up. Slowly, it moved down the dirt road away from the houses until it disappeared in the dusk.

With darkness fast approaching, Lanthito started back to the denning area where the other cubs were waiting. Once back in the company of his siblings, he began to expect that his mother would soon return as she had faithfully done so many times before.

Yet when hours went by and there was no sign of her, Lanthito and the other cubs became very restless. They had not eaten since the previous day when their mother had brought home a large redbird for them to feed upon. What could they do? And where could they go?

Should they wait for their mother's return? Or should they venture out into the cold January night in hopes of finding her?

More hours passed. The first glow of dawn saw the cubs huddled together asleep at the base of a big ponderosa. Bands of sunlight began to break above the eastern horizon and wash over the large granite boulders of the denning site. Lanthito was first to awaken. He gave a big yawn and looked around, yet he could see no sign of his mother. Roused by growing pangs of hunger, the other cubs also awoke, stretching and blinking.

The cubs' dilemma heightened. Should they wait for the return of their mother, or yield to the intensifying urge to strike out on their own? Finally, Lanthito could contain himself no longer. He

began to make his way down the side of the canyon, hopping from rock to rock. The other cubs followed. Where they were going and what they would find did not seem to matter. Their instincts told them they had to move.

After meandering around for several hours, Lanthito and the cubs found themselves farther down the canyon away from the denning area. Their bellies rumbling with hunger, they were keen to any odors that resembled something to eat. Scurrying through the patchy snow, the cubs came to a small draw and followed it up the ridge toward the back deck of a house. Concealed behind a growth of buck brush, Lanthito could see a two-legger standing in front of a large, black container from which billowed clouds of slow-rising smoke. The smoke definitely carried the odor of fresh meat. Lanthito's mouth started to water as he studied the scene before him with great interest.

The two-legger bent over the smoking vessel and scooped up several round, flat objects from it and put them on a platter. Then he went inside the house.

Attracted by the wafting aromas, Lanthito bravely but cautiously crept onto the deck. He sniffed at the wooden boards, which were spattered with drippings from the cooking meat. Hungrily, Lanthito began to lick the grease-ladened boards and the legs of the smoking pot, which were covered with little rivers of gravy. It was different than anything he had ever tasted, but it was good.

Suddenly he noticed something lying on the deck. One of the flat, round objects had apparently fallen from the two-legger's platter.

It was meat! In a flash Lanthito pounced on it and ran back toward the thicket of brush where he immediately began to devour it. The other cubs ran over to share in the find, but Lanthito would not allow it. His ears drew back and he hissed loudly at one of the cubs, who stopped and returned the display.

Sensing an opportunity, one of the other cubs attempted to scoop up the prize. There was a brief skirmish and pieces of meat flew in several directions. No sooner did the morsels hit the ground than they were gulped down by the famished cubs.

The noisy interaction of the cubs alerted a couple of neighborhood dogs who started to bark loudly. Frightened by the ruckus, the cubs scampered off to the safety of the forest.

The tiny bits of two-legger's meat were little more than appetizers for the cubs and seemed to make them even more aware of their hunger. But it was getting late in the day, and they instinctively started back toward the denning area. It was the one spot they associated most with food and they also knew it as a safe haven. In about a half hour the cubs arrived at the familiar outcropping of rocks. They curled up together for warmth and fell asleep. Lanthito began to dream of waking up in the morning to a big breakfast of redbird served up by his mother.

But morning came and there was no mother mountain lion nor redbird waiting. Lanthito leaped to the ground from a jumble of rocks and trotted back into the forest. The other cubs followed his lead, loping along behind him. Rounding a large Douglas fir tree, he stopped dead in his tracks. In front of him, not more than two feet away, crouched a large cottontail rabbit. For a split-second both of them stood rigid with surprise, gazing into each other's eyes. Then like a flash of lightning the cottontail rocketed away. Instinctively, Lanthito sprang into the chase. But, he was no challenge for the evasive lagomorph, who zigged and zagged through the underbrush leaving only the fleeting image of its cotton-white tail for the frustrated cub to ponder.

Excited by the chase, Lanthito and the cubs resumed their wanderings. As they entered a small glade surrounded by a grove of leafless aspens, Lanthito sensed a certain familiarity with the area. Also, there was the faint odor of something he had smelled before. He followed the scent to its source—a small pile of mountain lion droppings covered with dirt and pine needles. There were several such deposits which encircled a large mound composed of dirt, pine needles and twigs.

Then Lanthito remembered! This was the spot where his mother just a few nights ago had buried the dog carcass.

The cubs hurriedly scraped away the debris from the top of the mound and quickly began to devour the prey. Needless to say, they were very pleased to find this cache of food left behind by their mother, and ate until they were quite full.

Lanthito and the cubs were beginning to extend the range of their daily excursions through the forest. Each day they returned to feed on the dog carcass that their mother had cached for them. But, after about a week or so, only some bones were left.

Being the middle of winter, there were no chipmunks and ground squirrels to go after; these little rodents were deep in their burrows hibernating. And there were not too many birds around either; most of them had migrated to warmer climates. Besides, spotting a prey animal is

one thing; catching it is quite another matter.

Although Lanthito and the cubs had watched their mother catch redbirds and even a dog, they had never actually hunted by themselves. So once again, the cubs had to rely on whatever scraps of human food they chanced to find in the neighborhood.

One such hunger-ridden evening, just after dark, Lanthito and the cubs ventured toward the bottom of the canyon near the busy highway. The traffic was heavy with commuters heading back to their mountain homes after a long day's work in the city.

Attracted by a crumpled fast-food wrapper discarded by a passing motorist, one of the cubs, Lanthito's smaller brother, sallied over to the

edge of the roadway. Lanthito followed cautiously. But suddenly out of nowhere, the blinding headlights of a car appeared from around a sharp bend in the road.

The sound of rubber tires screeching across the pavement frightened Lanthito. He immediately turned and bolted back up the canyon, with his two sisters following close behind. As they crested a large boulder, they looked back toward the road expecting to see their brother scampering up behind them. But, he was not there. They peered further down the canyon. A moment later they saw him, sprawled out on the gravel shoulder of the highway. He wasn't moving.

They watched attentively, with their night-adapted, probing eyes.

The car that had frightened them had come to a stop. A two-legger got out and ran over to their brother. He picked up a stick and gently poked at the lifeless cub as though he were trying to rouse it. But their brother remained motionless. Suddenly, another car full of two-leggers pulled up to see what the matter was. They piled out and crowded around the little cub, seemingly quite interested in his appearance.

Lanthito remembered how the two-leggers had gathered around his mother shortly after he had heard the big noise, and how she merely lay there without moving. Now his brother also lay there quietly, unmoving. Both times unusual noises were involved and two-leggers were present. Lanthito was beginning to understand that two-leggers and their animals and their machines were sources of potential danger for him and his kind.

The climb back up the canyon was slow and uncertain. The cubs kept to a narrow draw that led them to the small meadow where their mother had left the food cache. But that food source had been gone for some time now.

Lanthito and his two sisters meandered about the ridge top for several more hours, until they finally nestled together in a large rock crevice and fell asleep. By the next morning, brisk gusts of wind from the west lashed over the rocky landscape and whined through the tips of the ponderosa pines. A winter storm was building up over the Continental Divide and would shortly deliver its load of dry, January snow to the foothills below. The three-week interlude of unseasonably warm weather was about to end. Sensing the sharp drop in temperature, the cubs huddled closer together to keep their collective heat from escaping.

Lanthito poked his little pink nose out of the rock crevice and felt the stab of the sharp, cold wind against it. He continued to sniff for a second or two and was about to pull his head back into the warmth of the small cave when he caught a whiff of a vaguely familiar aroma. He looked up to detect the origin of the pungent odor and saw in the distance a huge male mountain lion scraping together a small pile of dry grass, pine needles and twigs.

Lanthito watched as the long, black-tipped tail of the unusually large male swayed rhythmically back and forth as he ripped through the semi-frozen ground with inch-long, razor-sharp claws. With each powerful stroke of his forelegs the dense musculature of his massive shoulders bulged and rippled under his smooth, light-brown pelage. Periodically, the giant cat would stop and soak the pile with strong-smelling urine, which had wafted in Lanthito's direction.

Lanthito sat riveted at the awesome sight of the stately male and suddenly realized that he had seen this menacing animal before. Several weeks ago, early one morning, the big cat had rambled near the denning area. Detecting the intruder, Lanthito's mother quickly signaled the cubs to conceal themselves among the rocks. Then with a ferocious growl she sprinted over to the unwanted guest and attacked him. Taken completely by surprise, the gigantic male, who was nearly twice the size of Lanthito's mother, turned and ran away. Lanthito's mother remained quite tense and alert for the remainder of that day and kept the cubs hidden among the boulders. She made it quite clear to them that adult males of their kind were very dangerous and they should always remain hidden whenever one was near.

With Lanthito's mother no longer around for protection, the male had returned and was leaving his odorous boundary markers to announce his presence to all other mountain lions. Luckily, Lanthito and his sisters were downwind and remained undetected by the male. Had they been discovered it would have been certain death, for male mountain lions typically attack and kill younger members of the species that are not their own offspring.

Now, on top of everything else—lack of food, marauding dogs, careening cars and frigid weather—the cubs had to be on the alert for this newest threat to their survival.

Finally, the large male finished his marking behavior and headed slowly away. Lanthito and his sisters waited for a few more hours. Then when they could no longer ignore their hunger pangs, they left their protective haven and began again to search for food.

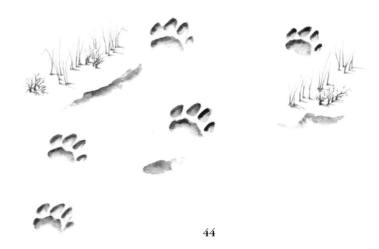

An abrupt nudge at my shoulder released me from my deep sleep and my entanglement with Lanthito's dream world. I turned my head to see what had caused this untimely disturbance. Tiki's large black foreleg was resting across my chest. His huge brown eyes, politely trained on me, carried the obvious message. "Hey, wake up, it's time for our walk."

I had managed to doze off for a good two hours and we were that long overdue for our nightly sojourn through the neighborhood. "Okay, okay, Mr. T., I get the picture, you'll have your walk," I responded.

I thought that as long as I had to go out into the night at this hour—nearly midnight—I might as well go and check the traps one more time. So, Tiki and I took off down Ridge Road.

It was an especially dark and moonless night. A partial cover of clouds blocked the usual star-lit sky. I could barely make out the road ahead of us, without the aid of my six-volt flashlight. Tiki knew the way and stayed a constant thirty feet in front of me, stopping at every intersection and cross path waiting for me to bring up the rear.

As we walked through the darkness toward the denning area, my thoughts returned to the dream I had just experienced. It was as though I had been able to venture into Lanthito's inner being and to obtain a quick but revealing glance of his situation. In a state of unconsciousness, my mind had taken various facts and events of the past few weeks and woven them together with other thin threads of knowledge residing in my brain to create a living tapestry. I somehow felt I had gained a bit more insight about what the cubs might be up against.

As we approached the side-road to the denning area where the traps were set, I put Tiki on his leash. If the cubs were near, I did not want him detecting their scent and running after them. The forest seemed to close in on us abruptly as we headed down the narrow dirt road. Suddenly, Tiki stopped dead in his tracks. Then ahead of us in a thicket of trees, I heard the crash of heavy footsteps thundering through the underbrush. Tiki began to growl and strain forcefully at the leash. It

was all I could do to hold back his powerful, tensed body. I turned the beam of my flashlight toward the direction of the noise, but could see nothing. I knew that whatever it was, it had to be big to smash through the forest like that.

Without warning a huge dark form jumped out in front of us. I pointed the flashlight at it and in full view, only about fifteen feet away, was a gigantic bull elk. "No, Tiki, stay!" I yelled, as he pulled even harder at the leash. In a split second the elk disappeared as it bulldozed its way through the undergrowth.

The elk and the noise gave me quite a start, and I was glad to have Tiki with me for moral support. Although, I'm sure he would have much rather enjoyed a good chase if I had let him.

After all the excitement was over, we hurried to the denning site to check the traps. No mountain lion cubs, as I expected.

On the way back down the side-road, where we had spooked the elk, I noticed a large pile of hay. One of the neighbors had apparently left it there to attract elk and deer onto the property. Some mountain residents put out food for large game during the winter so they can see

them from their homes.   Of course, the elk and deer can do quite well without this supplementary food source.   Furthermore, the more prey species like elk and deer there are in the area, the more mountain lions and other large predators move in.

The next morning I decided to get up early and drive out toward the denning area to check the traps again. This time I left Tiki at home, much to his obvious indignation. I parked my 4 x 4 Scout about half way down the side road leading to the traps, right near the spot where Tiki and I had flushed out the bull elk the night before.

Just above the trap-line was a very large formation of boulders, on top of which flew a rather tattered American flag. It was tied to a crooked pine branch, which served as a makeshift flagpole. This was the command headquarters of the neighborhood kid who liked to dress up in

army fatigues and play soldier in the woods. It was on his father's land that we had set the traps.

About two weeks ago, according to his dad, the intrepid little trooper was out on maneuvers when, quite unexpectedly, he came running home hollering and screaming in a terrible fright. "There's lions out there, I just saw some lions!" he shouted as his alarmed father came out to see what was the matter. It seems that the boy rounded a clump of bushes only to find himself face to face with Lanthito and the other cubs, who no doubt turned tail and ran away just as terrified as he was.

I climbed up to the top of the boulder pile and sat down next to the flagpole, being careful not to knock it over. From this position I had a good panorama of the canyon, and was able to see nearly all of the traps through my 10 x 50 binoculars.

One by one I spied the traps with great anticipation; but, one by one they came up empty. As I scanned the terrain in search of the last couple of traps, my field glasses filled with three little figures. "I'll be darned," I said under my breath, "it's the cubs!"

They were moving quietly along the contour of the ridge toward the denning site. As they approached, Lanthito, who was in the lead, noticed one of the live-traps.

His curiosity obviously aroused, Lanthito walked closer to inspect the strange contraption. Crouched low to the ground, his body fully extended, he stuck his head into the opening of the trap to get a better look. At the far end of the trap was a large lump of cat food. Its strong, fishy odor made Lanthito's nostrils quiver with excitement. He lengthened his body further into the trap, carefully and slowly, but still he could not quite reach the bait. Finally, Lanthito took a small step forward. Unknowingly, he placed his foot on the metal trigger plate. With a loud "wang!" the trap door slammed shut, smacking Lanthito in the rear end. Startled, he arched his back and gave out a powerful hiss, exposing an impressive set of sharp teeth.

There was hardly any room in the trap to turn around, but with difficulty, Lanthito managed to do so, only to find that the entrance was blocked by the trap door. Aroused and frightened, Lanthito frantically searched for a way out, biting the cage, scratching at the wires. But to no avail. After a minute or so of initial panic, he settled down.

Lanthito's attention quickly refocused on his hunger and on the gob of cat food that also occupied the trap. So, accepting his new predicament for the moment, he proceeded to eat up the bait with great pleasure, licking every last bit of mouth-watering flavor from the floor of the trap.

All the while, Lanthito's sisters sat and watched the goings-on with apparent interest. They, too, were no doubt attracted by the pungent odor of the cat food, but it was Lanthito who took the initiative and got to it first. However, now he was paying the price for taking the risk. And I had finally caught him!

Lanthito's sisters circled around the trap occasionally licking him through the wire mesh. Finally, they snuggled up next to their caged brother and waited.

I ran back to my vehicle and grabbed a large blanket, then hurriedly

returned to the traps. A wide expanse of snow separated me from the cubs. I immediately drew their attention as I crunched my way through it. The cubs froze in place. Lanthito seemed to suddenly become conscious of his utter entrapment. With no way to protect himself or to escape, he began to show obvious signs of alarm, arching his back, baring his teeth and retracting his ears.

As I appeared in full view from behind a stand of trees, Lanthito's sisters sat up and peered in my direction, wanting to flee, but at the same time wanting to remain close to Lanthito.

It was a moment of great panic for Lanthito as I approached near the trap. His sisters remained near their imprisoned brother as long as their instincts to flee would allow, then took off in a gallop.

Lanthito scrambled violently to escape, clawing and biting at the hard, unassailable walls of the live-trap. He hissed and growled at me. I quickly crouched over the trap and covered it with the blanket in order to conceal myself from his view.

Climbing back up the side of the steep canyon carrying a heavy metal live-trap containing a rather disgruntled twenty-five pound mountain lion cub was no easy task. After fifty yards or so, Lanthito finally settled down. I could feel the power of his sinewy grip as he grasped tightly to the floor of the trap with his extended claws.

Finally, I made it back to the Scout, panting heavily from the long ascent. I carefully placed the trap in the back of my rig keeping it entirely covered with the blanket. Off I sped over the bumpy, gravel road back to my cabin.

As I rolled up the driveway, Tiki came out of the woods to greet me as he typically does. I said to myself, "Now this is going to be interesting. Wait until he sees who I've got with me."

It took only a second for Tiki to determine that things were not smelling the same as usual. He immediately became quite alert and brusquely goggled into the cab of the Scout as I opened the door to exit. I went to the back of the Scout and unlatched the tail gate. Tiki was almost beside himself with inquisitiveness, rapidly glancing back and forth at me and then the large, blanket-covered object in the rear of the Scout. He seemed to be saying, "Okay, okay, what's in there, come on, let me in on it, too."

I dragged the enshrouded trap to the edge of the tail gate and pulled back the blanket just enough for Tiki to look inside. He sniffed at the trap, his big black nose trembling with excitement. On the other side of the wire mesh, not two inches away was Lanthito. Eyes transfixed on each other, Tiki and Lanthito stood motionless, as though they were statues in granite. Then with eyes still glued to Lanthito, Tiki slowly backed away from the trap and looked at me rather approvingly. I readjusted the blanket over the small opening and carried the trap into the cabin.

Once inside the cabin, I transferred Lanthito to a large holding cage, which I had covered with a big, pink afghan—a gift from one of my aunts, which I had finally put to good use. The transfer was easier than I had anticipated. First I covered the holding cage, myself, and the entrapped cub with a heavy nylon net, just in case anything went wrong. I didn't want to take any chances of having a wild mountain lion, even a small one, loose in my cabin. Then I placed the trap inside the holding cage, slowly pulled back the cover and opened the spring door of the trap. I made sure that it was darkest at the far end of the holding cage by positioning and adjusting the lights in my basement just so. And that's exactly where Lanthito headed, but not without first giving me a couple of well-deserved hisses and growls in the process.

An hour passed; the excitement of his new experiences apparently tired Lanthito out. He finished the cat food I had placed in the holding cage, then curled up in a corner and fell asleep.

Although quite elated to have caught Lanthito, I was concerned about Lanthito's sisters, who were still on the loose. The weather was rapidly worsening and I knew they had nothing to eat. Their chances of survival were slim. So, I decided to go back to the traps, hoping that the other two cubs had returned to the area.

I walked slowly and as silently as I could toward the top of the boulder pile where I could see all of the traps. When I looked below me I could hardly believe my eyes. There were Lanthito's sisters, each one sitting quietly in a trap. The temptation of the cat food was just too much. They too had taken the bait and had been captured.

Back at the cabin, Lanthito and his sisters were reunited in the holding cage. The transfer technique that I had devised for Lanthito also worked for his sisters, but it was somewhat of a nervous situation for all of the cubs. They jostled for position and swiped at each other with their paws. I was the object of their fear and aggression, which they redirected toward each other, given the close confinement of the holding cage. But things quickly settled down once the transfer was completed, the lights were turned off, and I disappeared from view. They devoured more cat food and drank a lot of water, and then all snuggled up together in a big heap and fell asleep.

The next morning I rather reluctantly telephoned the wildlife authorities to come and pick up the cubs and transport them to the rehabilitation center. I was wishing I could keep the cubs for awhile longer to observe their interesting behavior, but I knew how important it was to get them to their new home as soon as possible.

The ranger arrived and we loaded the holding cage onto the bed of his truck. As the truck pulled away, I felt both a sense of relief and of sadness. I was very sorry to see them go. Lanthito and his sisters had ended one exciting chapter in their lives, and certainly so had I. What lay ahead for them, no one really knew. But at least for the moment, they were warm and fed and together.

That evening, as the events of the day began to wear off, I sat next to my glowing, potbelly stove to enter some notes in my field journal. I started to write, "February 17, 1991...." Then I suddenly realized it was my birthday. I thought to myself, what a wonderful birthday present I had received; three feisty mountain lion cubs, right here in my own cabin for a night. What unlikely houseguests. Never in my wildest dreams would I have expected such a fantastic gift. Truly, it's a birthday I'll always remember.

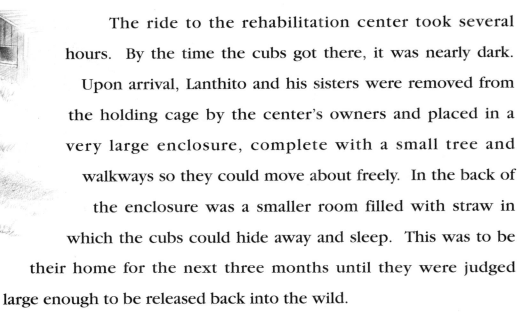

The ride to the rehabilitation center took several hours. By the time the cubs got there, it was nearly dark. Upon arrival, Lanthito and his sisters were removed from the holding cage by the center's owners and placed in a very large enclosure, complete with a small tree and walkways so they could move about freely. In the back of the enclosure was a smaller room filled with straw in which the cubs could hide away and sleep. This was to be their home for the next three months until they were judged large enough to be released back into the wild.

The rehabilitation center is operated by a husband and wife team who are actually school teachers by profession. They live in a remote valley west of Pueblo, Colorado and, with great dedication, spend nearly all of their spare time taking care of injured and abandoned wild animals and nursing them back to health. Lanthito and his sisters were in very capable hands during their stay there.

By design, they were kept away from people as much as possible during their confinement. Their large cage was actually housed in an open shed, which allowed them plenty of sunshine during the day, but also afforded them some measure of privacy. The idea was to make as little visual contact with them as possible.

It was also important for the cubs not to associate humans as providers of food, so that after their release, they would not seek out areas inhabited by people for a free handout. At the rehabilitation center they were fed mainly road kills—deer, rabbits, squirrels—which were brought in by the wildlife rangers. The carcasses were left in the front part of the large cage during the night when the cubs were asleep in the rear compartment. Feeding on wild game allowed them to become acquainted with the smells and tastes of the natural food they would eventually be capturing and eating in the wild.

Occasionally, a live rodent was released in the cub's enclosure. It was quickly and instinctively dispatched and eaten. This was done to help hone the cub's hunting skills, which they would normally have learned over a long period of time—up to eighteen months—by accompanying their mother on hunts.

Finally, in late May, over four months since their mother had been killed, the wildlife experts decided that Lanthito and his sisters were ready for release. By now they had reached the status of sub-adult mountain lions and could presumably fend for themselves in their natural habitat.

In order to be removed from the cage and transported to the release site, Lanthito and his sisters had to be tranquilized. While they were asleep, they were weighed, measured and also fitted with small

yellow ear tags for future identification if they ever happened to be seen again. Lanthito was over five feet long and weighed in at sixty-four pounds. His sisters were a few inches shorter and several pounds lighter.

Before they had a chance to wake up, the young mountain lions were loaded into an enclosed trailer built to transport wild animals. Then they were driven to a remote area in southern Colorado chosen by the wildlife authorities because of its isolation from humans. Also, there was plenty of wild game there—turkeys, ground squirrels, snowshoe hares, grouse, deer and elk—as well as water.

The journey to the release site ended in a beautiful mountain meadow full of wildflowers. It was ringed by thick stands of ponderosa pine. By now Lanthito and his sisters had fully recovered from the immobility caused by the tranquilizer. The wildlife ranger climbed up on the trailer and lifted the sliding door. Immediately, Lanthito leaped out and bolted across the meadow taking long powerful strides as he headed swiftly to the edge of the forest. His sisters quickly followed.

When he reached the cover of the pine trees, Lanthito briefly stopped and looked back toward the ranger and his congenial keepers of the past few months. The glance could almost be construed by the on-looking "two-leggers" as a small acknowledgment of thanks. Then he quickly disappeared from view.

And so began another episode in this true-life adventure. Just how well Lanthito and his sisters will be able to do on their own as young mountain lions raised in captivity, we will probably never know for sure. Their will to survive is great, or they would have never made it this far. But, I would like to think that with Lanthito leading the way, their chances of learning how to readjust to their new natural surroundings are very, very good, indeed.

Epilogue

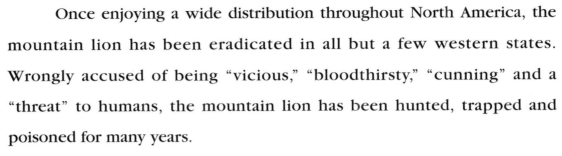

Once enjoying a wide distribution throughout North America, the mountain lion has been eradicated in all but a few western states. Wrongly accused of being "vicious," "bloodthirsty," "cunning" and a "threat" to humans, the mountain lion has been hunted, trapped and poisoned for many years.

As we all know, it is not just this species that has suffered. Entire ecosystems—forests, grasslands, wetlands—have been drastically altered and even destroyed because of our mistakes and our misunderstanding of nature.

As humans continue to encroach on the habitat of the mountain lion, the number of encounters between these two competing species will increase. Inevitably, and unfairly, humans will probably prevail.

As for the story of Lanthito and his family, it has probably been repeated many times throughout recent history. Unfortunately, it may continue to recur until humans, as the "intelligent species," realize that mountain lions and other large predators are very important components of natural ecosystems.

Ironically, as we cause the extinction of more and more species, humans are the ones who will ultimately suffer the most. Many people— scientists, politicians and ordinary citizens—are beginning to understand this and—before it's too late—do something about it. The first step is demanding better and more acceptable ways to manage the mountain lion and other wildlife.

But before any real progress can be made, perhaps we need to develop a respect and an appreciation for all other species and for nature, just as the original North Americans must have had. After all, they were able to live in relative harmony with the mountain lion and other large predators for thousands of years.

Wildlife biologists are in agreement that there is still a great deal to learn about the behavior and ecology of the mountain lion, especially as it relates to human interactions. However, the greatest challenge we face in understanding this much maligned and mistreated species is, first and foremost, to understand ourselves and our rightful place in the natural scheme of things. Then, and only then, will we be able to justly and honorably resolve the complex issues surrounding humans and mountain lions.

————

In March of 1992 one of the cubs was sighted on a ranch in northern New Mexico about forty miles from the release site. According to the report, the cub was treed by some hunters' dogs. Alerted by the cub's yellow ear tags, the hunters called off their dogs and reported the

sighting to the owner of the ranch, who in turn informed the wildlife authorities. The cub appeared to be healthy and in very good condition.

So, we know for sure that at least one of the cubs made it through the winter. And I think it's safe to say that if one did, then the likelihood that the others also survived is also very high.

While the cubs may remain together for a while, even hunting together, they are ultimately solitary and will eventually go their separate ways.

Other Reading On Mountain Lions

Hansen, Kevin. 1992. Cougar: The American Lion. Northland Publishing and the Mountain Lion Foundation, Sacramento, California.

Robinson, Sandra C. 1991. Mountain Lion. Roberts Rinehart Publishers, Niwot, Colorado.

Shaw, Harley. 1989. Soul Among Lions: The Cougar as Peaceful Adversary. Johnson Books, Boulder, Colorado.